CW00336223

THE LOST EPISTLES

THE LOST EPISTLES

LETTERS TO THE FAITHFUL
IN THE EARLY CHURCH

Edited by
Robert Van de Weyer

ARTHUR JAMES
EVESHAM

Published in 1996 by Arthur James Ltd.
4 Broadway Road, Evesham, Worcestershire, WR11 6BH

ISBN 0-85305-356-1

Typeset in Bembo by Little Gidding Books.
Printed and bound in Great Britain by Biddles Ltd, Guildford.

PREFACE

The original community at Little Gidding was founded in 1626 by Nicholas Ferrar; their beautiful chapel continues to attract numerous visitors. A new community formed in the late 1970s; and, like its predecessor, it includes families and single people, following a simple rule and pattern of prayer.

Little Gidding Books is the publishing arm of the community. In addition to its Prayer Book it publishes each quarter a book of daily readings, and each year a set of readings and meditations for the festival weeks and Lent. These sets of readings may be used in conjunction with the Prayer Book, or on their own. They are supplied directly to Friends of Little Gidding, and are also available to the wider public through bookshops.

The community is dedicated to Christ the Sower; hence its symbol is a cross made from ears of corn. The hand in which 'Little Gidding Books' is written on the cover is that of Nicholas Ferrar – the words have been taken from his letters.

If you would like to have more information, please write to:

The Community of Christ the Sower
Little Gidding
Huntingdon
PE17 5RJ
United Kingdom

INTRODUCTION

Christianity is now an ancient religion, encrusted by tradition; so it is difficult for us today to recapture the youthful vitality of the first Christian congregations. And the epistles of Paul and Peter, John and James, addressed to those communities, are so familiar to us, and so burdened by layers of interpretation, that we can easily miss the passionate vigour with which the words were composed. Yet the death of the first apostles did not mark the end of this particular form of spiritual communication. On the contrary, Christian leaders continued to write epistles which – like those of Paul and the rest – were intended to be read aloud at public worship. And these epistles were copied, and then passed eagerly from one Christian congregation to another. Once the canon of Scripture was agreed late in the second century, and these later epistles excluded, they were largely lost from sight, studied only by scholars. Thus when we encounter them today they are as fresh – and as hard-hitting – as they were to those who first heard them two millennia ago. And we can enter anew the hearts and minds of Christians at a time when the faith was young and novel.

The earliest of these forgotten epistles come from Clement who was leader of the congregation in Rome in the last decade of the first century – less than thirty years after the apostle Peter was martyred there. He had probably been a slave in a Christian household, in which the husband was martyred by Nero; and after his own conversion had been set free. His letter to the church in Corinth was prompted by news reaching Rome that, as in Paul's time, the Corinthian Christians were divided, with rival groups following different leaders. Clement was not a great theologian, nor a man of passion, but saw Christianity primarily as a moral movement, whose central feature should be the pure and holy lives of its believers. In writing to Corinth he was not asserting the dominance of Rome, but he saw himself as a loving brother offering advice. The second letter ascribed to Clement may be by a later hand, but the same tone and attitude continue.

Ignatius was bishop of the Syrian city of Antioch – where, according to the Book of Acts, the believers were first called Christians – in the first decade of the second century. He was tried and condemned to death in his own city, but taken to Rome to be thrown to the wild beasts in the amphitheatre. During the long journey under guard through Asia Minor, Christians from throughout the province came to meet him. He in turn wrote letters of greetings and encouragement for them to take back to their churches. He also wrote to the church in Rome to warn of his impending arrival. His letters reveal a nervous, anxious man, lacking social grace, and yet filled with spiritual joy. His central concern is the unity of the church, and the danger of division; and he stressed the role of the bishop as a focus of unity and discipline. He has often been quoted over the centuries by the advocates of strict authority in the church.

Polycarp was Bishop of Smyrna for the first fifty years of the second century; and he was a friend and correspondent of Ignatius – as his own epistle testifies. He came from a patrician family, and was respected throughout the city, by non-believers as well as his flock, for his wisdom and unfailing courtesy. As a young man he had been a disciple of John the Divine, author of the Book of Revelation. He lived to a great age, and in 155 fell victim to a local persecution. His letter to the Philippian Church contains few special insights, but reflects his gracious personality.

The epistle of Barnabas has traditionally been ascribed to the Barnabas who was a companion of Paul. But there was a custom at this time (examples of which are found in the New Testament itself) of writers adopting the name of a figure whom they seek to emulate. So in fact the author of this work is unknown. Judging by the ideas contained in the epistle he may have lived in Alexandria, and was certainly influenced by the philosophical ideas of that city which drew a sharp dividing-line between the Judaism of the Old Testament and the gospel of Christ. The date is probably some time in the first three decades of the second century.

The anonymous letter to Diognetus is the earliest surviving example of 'apologetics', in which the writer attempts to justify the Christian faith before the pagan world. In the first century the main concern of the church was to win converts and establish some form of organisation. But by the middle decades of the second century Christianity had become a major religious element in many Roman cities, attracting wealthy and educated converts as well as the poor and dispossessed. Thus the authorities grew increasingly hostile, and local persecutions became more frequent and bloody. Scholarly Christians, such as the writer of this letter, responded by trying to show that Christianity was rational and also constituted no threat to civil order; indeed they argued that in practice the high moral standards of Christians would make the task of government easier. The exact date of the epistle is uncertain, with some scholars putting it as early as about AD 120.

In truth most readers of the New Testament epistles are quite selective, enjoying the more accessible parts, and mentally setting on one side the large chunks which do not relate to the modern mind. The forgotten epistles contain even larger obscure chunks, so this book is highly selective. Like the strictures of Paul and Peter, the teaching contained in these epistles is tough and uncompromising, and often quite disturbing; but that is the nature of the Christian faith – or, at least, should be.

Robert Van de Weyer

1

I apologize for the delay in dealing with the issues disputed amongst you, and especially the alien ideas which a few rash and self-willed people amongst you have been spreading. Once you were renowned for the peace and good will that reigned within your community; but now that reputation is sullied by your bitter conflicts. Who amongst your guests has not testified to your virtues and your steadfast faith? Who has not admired your seriousness of purpose and your quiet piety? Who has not reported your generous hospitality? Who has not blessed your profound wisdom? You acted always without regard for personal status, but did only what was righteous in the eyes of God. You taught your children the simple and gentle ways of Christ. Your womenfolk were blameless and pure, showing warm affection for their husbands. And your menfolk were humble, free of all arrogance, and always more ready to give than to receive.

First Epistle of Clement to the Corinthians

2

The Holy Spirit was poured out in abundance on you all, giving you a rich and profound sense of peace, and also an insatiable desire to do good. You were full of holy plans, and with childlike trust you opened your arms to God, praying to him for all your needs. Day and night you strove to add to the number of God's elect, urging those around you to submit to his mercy and compassion. You were utterly sincere, with no guile, and bore no malice towards one another. As if by instinct you rejected any ideas foreign to the truth, and conflict was unthinkable. You mourned over the misery and the sin of your neighbours, as if that misery and sin belonged to you. And you offered help to your neighbours without any thought of the cost to you. You were true citizens of God's kingdom, and his laws were written on your hearts.

First Epistle of Clement to the Corinthians

3

Out of the perfect harmony which you enjoyed, there arose jealousy, envy, strife and disorder, with each group striving to undermine the others. The leaders of each faction are not men of virtue and holiness, but those who desire only power for themselves. The foolish have taken charge of the wise, the sinful have become masters of the righteous, the young have risen up against the old. Righteousness and peace have disappeared from your midst; you no longer fear God, but instead walk in paths of your own choosing, proudly trusting in your own strength; the eye of faith has grown dim within you. Once you were citizens of God's kingdom, worthy to be brothers and sisters of his Son; now you are citizens of the world. Once you were ready to be Christ's bride; now you are married to envy and wickedness.

First Epistle of Clement to the Corinthians

4

Let us remember two men who have recently fought long and hard in the battle between good and evil. Peter lost faith under trial, and deserted the path of righteousness; but his faith returned, and he testified to numerous people of the glorious mercy of God. Paul persecuted the faithful, but then found his way to the path of God. Seven times he was chained, exiled and stoned; yet he remained true to his vocation as a herald of the gospel across the world, and his noble faith became famous from the East to the West. He talked to rulers and to peasants with equal respect and passion, desiring only to open their hearts to God's truth. Peter and Paul are both wonderful examples to us of how wickedness can be overcome, and righteousness reign; and both are now taken up to the Holy Place which is their just reward.

First Epistle of Clement to the Corinthians

5

I am writing not just to admonish you, but also to renew my own strength, because we are all fighting in the same arena, and the same choices confront us. So let us put aside all new ideas which are foreign to our faith, and concentrate only on what we know to be true – and then let us do only what is good and pleasing in the eyes of our Maker. Let us fix our gaze on the blood of Christ, reminding ourselves how precious is that blood to his Father, because it was poured out for our salvation, and opened the door of repentance to the whole human race. Let us remember that even before the death of God's Son there have been men and women who have repented of their sins, and turned to God. Whenever a person has truly repented and prayed to God for forgiveness, God has answered their prayer. In generation after generation, since time began, aliens and enemies of God have become faithful and righteous followers.

First Epistle of Clement to the Corinthians

6

It is right and holy, my brothers, to obey God rather than to follow those who out of pride and lust for power poison us with jealousy. We shall suffer no ordinary harm, but put ourselves in the most terrible danger, if we submit to the schemes of men who relish strife and division, and who peddle their own ideas rather than the teachings of Christ and his holy apostles. Let us be kind and considerate to one another, imitating the compassion and sweetness of our Master. And let us hold fast to those leaders amongst us whose words reflect only the words of Christ, and whose desire for harmony is utterly sincere. For Christ belongs to those who are humble in heart and mind, not to those who try to exalt themselves over his flock. The sceptre of his kingship is made not of pomp and pride, but of simplicity and gentleness and the desire to serve others.

First Epistle of Clement to the Corinthians

7

Let us fix our eyes on the Father and Creator of the whole world, and hold fast to his excellent gifts of peace and love. Let us contemplate his purposes in creation, and consider how free from all anger he is towards his creatures. The moon and stars move in harmony as he has ordered; day and night follow the course fixed by him without hindering each other. The earth teems with all kinds of creatures, and gives food in abundance for all as he has ordained. The sea is gathered in the places he has chosen and does not break through the shore and flood the dry land. The seasons of spring, summer, autumn and winter give way to one another in peace. The winds blow from north, east, south and west as he calls them, and springs of water break through the rocks to supply drink for animals and men. God in all his creation willed that there should be perfect peace and concord. And when humanity fell into sin, bringing conflict and misery, he sent his Son Jesus Christ to restore peace.

First Epistle of Clement to the Corinthians

8

If God has ordained perfect harmony throughout the world, then we must live together in harmony. Remember how near God is to us; he knows all our thoughts and our plans, because nothing escapes his attention. So we should not defy his will. Instead we should defy those foolish and thoughtless men who are puffed up with their own eloquence, taking pride in their own words rather than God's words. Let us honour the old, let us instruct the young in the fear of God, and let us lead one another in the ways of righteousness. Let our womenfolk wear the beautiful cloak of purity and let them cover their heads with innocence; let their tongues be free of malicious gossip, but let them show love to all who love God. Let our children learn the strength which comes from humility before God, and let them discover how beautiful is the gift of salvation which he offers. And let our menfolk always be diligent in seeking truth, and let the breath of the Holy Spirit inspire their every word and action.

First Epistle of Clement to the Corinthians

9

Let us consider, beloved, how God continually proves to us that there will be a resurrection, of which he has made our Lord Jesus Christ the first fruits by raising him from the dead. We need only look at the signs of resurrection all around us. When the dawn comes each morning, it is the rising of the day from the sleep of night. When a seed falls on the ground it must first die, before rising to life and growing into a sturdy plant. Is it not a great and wonderful thing that the Creator of the universe will bring about the resurrection of all who have served him in holiness, and trust in his love? In this hope let our souls bind themselves to him who is faithful in his promises and righteous in his judgements. He who has commanded us not to lie shall not be a liar himself; for nothing is impossible for God except to lie. So day by day let our faith in him be rekindled, and let us remember that he loves and sustains all his creatures. In that love he will fulfil his promise that we shall share the risen life of his Son.

First Epistle of Clement to the Corinthians

10

Since all things are seen and heard by God, let us fear him, and reject all foul desire and evil schemes. We can never flee from his mighty hand, so let that hand bless us with a righteous heart. Thus we can approach him in true holiness, to share in his holiness. This means that we should never allow our tongues to speak evil of others. We should avoid drunkenness. Adultery should be so loathsome to us as to be unthinkable. We should destroy all personal pride and ambition. And we should avoid the company of evil people, recognising that in our weakness and frailty we can easily be influenced by their false words. Instead we should seek the company of those whose faith is firm, whose love is strong, and whose words can lead us only towards God's throne. Rather than prove ourselves, we should always prove God. Rather than draw attention to ourselves, we should point to the good deeds of others. In all things let gentleness and humility be our rulers.

First Epistle of Clement to the Corinthians

11

Let us think of ourselves as an army, with Christ as our general giving faultless commands. Those who are senior officers have a duty to ensure good order, and to train those under them for battle. And each person in the army must act according to the rank he has been given. Not everyone can be a prefect or a tribune or a centurion, but each must take his place in the chain of command. The great cannot exist without the small, nor the small without the great. Soldiers depend on each other, and an army can only be victorious if the soldiers fight together like a single body. So let us always look to Christ, our general, as the source of authority. Let us be obedient to those whom Christ has appointed as our pastors. And let us carry out our duties with diligence. In this way the strong will help the weak, and the weak will serve the strong. The rich will care for the poor, and the poor will pray for the rich. The wise man will guide those new to the faith, and the new convert will inspire the wise with their zeal.

First Epistle of Clement to the Corinthians

12

God, who imposed perfect order and harmony in the universe, has commanded us to worship. Thus we should obey his command, displaying his order and harmony in our services. We should meet for worship at fixed times, all arriving punctually. Our pastors should ensure that everything is conducted with piety and decorum. And we should each play the part assigned to us with care. There should be no dispute amongst you as to who should play what part. You yourselves have chosen your pastors, so they hold their position by common consent. They in turn have the right and the duty to discern each person's gifts, and to determine their part accordingly. Thus you must obey your pastors without rancour or argument. Remember that your pastors carry a heavy load of responsibility. Blessed be those pastors who have finished their work on earth, and can be released from this life, for then they shall be free of all evil plots to remove them from office.

First Epistle of Clement to the Corinthians

13

You are eager and zealous, beloved brethren, for the things which lead to salvation. You have studied the holy Scriptures, which are true and given by the Holy Spirit. You know that nothing unjust and false is written in them. Certainly the righteous were often persecuted, but only by those whose hearts were black with evil. The righteous were put in prison, they were stoned, and some were even killed. But through their suffering they held fast to God, and so by endurance gained his eternal reward. We for our part must follow their example. Yet, if you are so familiar with the holy Scriptures, why is there conflict and bitterness amongst you? Why do you tear yourselves asunder? What is this madness that threatens your hope of salvation? The divisions between you are turning you away from the path of righteousness. You must show the same endurance in the face of evil that our forefathers showed; like them you must cling only to what is true and good. That alone can restore your hope of salvation.

First Epistle of Clement to the Corinthians

14

Look again at the letters written to you by the blessed Paul the apostle. What did he write to you at the beginning of his preaching? With true inspiration he charged you with already creating parties and factions, some declining allegiance to him, others to Apollos, others to Cephas. Now consider the men who have perverted you, turning your hearts away from peace and concord. It is shameful, utterly shameful, and unworthy of your training in Christ, that by the false schemes and words of just a few men you are being disloyal to your true pastors. Report of your divisions is now spreading throughout the world, destroying your reputation amongst your fellow disciples. Put an end to this. Fall down before your Master, and with tears in your eyes beg him to forgive you and to reconcile you one with another, and so restore love amongst you. This will open again for you the gate of righteousness. Be wise in your words, and pure in your deeds, and humble in your hearts.

First Epistle of Clement to the Corinthians

15

Let him who loves Christ perform the commandments of Christ. Who is able to explain the bond of divine love? Who is able to describe its supreme beauty? The height to which love lifts us can never be expressed. Love unites us to God, and in the perfection of love words are useless. Who is able to experience love except those to whom God has granted it? Let us beg and pray that he may bestow on us the gift of love. Then all notion of parties and factions will melt away, and mutual recrimination will cease. The power of God's loving forgiveness will blot out the memory of past bitterness, and we shall know only the sweetness of perfect peace. Our minds and our mouths shall become incapable of guile and deceit, and only honest words shall be spoken. Such a wonderful blessing is given to all who commit themselves to God through our Lord Jesus Christ.

First Epistle of Clement to the Corinthians

16

Let us pray that for our transgressions, and for all the evil we have done, forgiveness may be granted to us. And let those who have been the leaders of the parties and factions within your church reflect carefully on their wrongdoings, and be reconciled to God and to one another. Those who live in the fear and love of God prefer to be tortured themselves rather than let their neighbours suffer, and they are willing to take blame upon themselves rather than let divisions persist. All of you, and especially the faction leaders, must let your hard hearts soften, so that you can accept the blame for the wrong you have done, and suffer the torture of humiliation. Confess your sins openly, without trying to hide anything, and then harmony will be restored amongst you. Who amongst you has the courage to do that? Let those people cry out: 'If I have caused strife and division, let me be punished; if I have led others in the path of evil, let me take the lowest place and perform only the most menial tasks.' Such people shall win for themselves great glory – the glory of being true disciples of Christ.

First Epistle of Clement to the Corinthians

17

In admonishing you for your transgressions, I am not seeking any power over you. I do not want you to submit to my authority, but to the authority of God, seeking to obey his will in humility and meekness. With all my heart I am praying for you, asking him to guide you. And if you can allow yourselves to be corrected by me, then you shall learn to receive correction from one another, for you are guardians of each other's souls. If we can be honest and frank with one another, gently pointing out sins without any spirit of moral pride, then we shall together be united with God's will. The only human authority which you must accept is that of the pastors, whom you yourselves have chosen. They have a particular duty to correct you, and to them you must bend the knees of your hearts. Never be boastful or haughty towards them, but submissive. Remember that the best position to hold with the church is not the highest but the lowliest.

First Epistle of Clement to the Corinthians

18

Let us pray with eager hearts to the Creator of the Universe, that he may number us amongst those who are to be saved, calling us from darkness to light, from ignorance to the full knowledge of his glory. Heavenly Father, source of all creation, open the eyes of our hearts to know you, for you are the highest of the high, the holiest of the holy. You can destroy the evil schemes of kings and emperors; you can raise up the lowly, and humble the proud; you can make the rich poor and the poor rich; you can choose the time of a person's birth and death; you can see all the works and the thoughts of men; you can rescue those in danger, encourage those in despair, comfort those who are sick; and you can save souls who are imprisoned by evil. All this you are able to accomplish through your beloved child, Jesus Christ, who has revealed to us your ways, and made us holy. Father, use your almighty power on our behalf. Have mercy on us, heal our diseases, strengthen us in our weakness, feed us in our hunger, and save us from all evil, through Jesus Christ our Lord.

First Epistle of Clement to the Corinthians

19

It is tempting to think little about Jesus Christ, and to concentrate almost all our attention on practical affairs. Equally it is tempting to think little of our salvation, and to have little concern for our sins, regarding them as trifles. Yet Jesus bore great suffering for our sakes, because he regarded our sins as so important, and because he so deeply desired our salvation. So how can we repay our huge debt to him? He gave us the light, he called us God's sons and daughters, he saved us when we were perishing. What praise should we give him in return for what we have received? We were ignorant, we were worshipping blocks of stones, ornaments of wood, statues of gold and silver, the works of men, and our whole life was nothing but death; and he showed us the way to worship the true and only God. He called us out of nothing into divine reality. How can we make ourselves worthy of this calling?

Second Epistle of Clement to the Corinthians

20

To repay our debt to Jesus Christ, we must first be willing to speak openly of him, confessing him as Lord and Master. And secondly we must do what he says, obeying his commandments, so that we honour him not only with our lips but with our hearts and our minds and our bodies. It is not sufficient merely to call him Lord; this is just the beginning. We must prove our words by loving one another, by not committing adultery, by not speaking one against the other, by not being jealous, but being self-controlled, merciful and good. We should have compassion for one another, seeking to help one another rather than pursue money and wealth for ourselves. And we must not fear men, but only fear God. Remember that we are just travellers through this world, on our journey to God's heavenly kingdom, so we should have no worldly attachments or ambitions. Be assured that our sojourn in the world is trivial, its pains and pleasures of little importance, and it lasts only a short time. But the heavenly kingdom which Christ promises is great and wonderful beyond our imagination, and lasts forever.

Second Epistle of Clement to the Corinthians

21

This world and the world to come are enemies. This world speaks of adultery, corruption, love of money and deceit. But the world to come bids these things farewell. We cannot be friends of both; instead we choose one or the other. It is surely wiser to hate the things of this world, for they are short-lived and soon decay, and to love the eternal things of the world to come. To become friends of the world to come means that we enter a contest, of which the prize is the crown of God's glory. To win this contest means to run through this life along an absolutely straight path, obeying without compromise the commandments of Christ. If we try to cheat, if we deviate from the straight line, then we put ourselves in danger of losing the contest, and condemning ourselves to everlasting misery. What do you think? Do you want to be a friend of the world to come? Do you wish to enter the contest and to win the prize?

Second Epistle of Clement to the Corinthians

22

We are like clay in the hands of the potter. If when he is making a vessel it breaks or bends in his hand, he can remodel it; but once he has put it into the kiln, there is nothing he can do to mend it. So while we are in the world, God can remodel us, if we repent and put ourselves at his mercy; he will make our hearts and our souls perfect, without fault or flaw. But once we have departed this world, we have entered the kiln of eternity: we can no longer repent and confess our sins, and then be remodelled. So let us repent while we are still on this earth, and then let us keep ourselves pure. While we still have the opportunity let us offer ourselves to God to be healed and made whole. But remember, repentance requires a sincere heart: we must be completely honest with God in confessing our sins, and honest in our intentions to obey the commandments of Christ.

Second Epistle of Clement to the Corinthians

23

There are two churches. The first is the spiritual church, which was created before the sun and the moon; the second is the visible church on earth. The church to which Christ calls us is the spiritual church, which is the community of all who are saved. This church is truly the body of Christ. As the Scriptures tell us it belongs not to the present world, but to the world to come; and when Christ came to earth, he revealed in his body the existence of this spiritual church, and invited us to join it. The visible church on earth is a kind of shadow of the spiritual church. It belongs to this world, yet it reflects and echoes the spiritual church which belongs to the world to come. Membership of the visible church is guarantee of salvation; yet through membership we can be led towards the spiritual church. But the visible church can always fall into corruption and sin; and when that happens we must keep ourselves pure, by holding fast to the spiritual church.

Second Epistle of Clement to the Corinthians

24

Those who exalt themselves over their flocks like to imagine that, owing to their higher status, they are closer to Christ. In fact the very opposite is true. Christ is closest to the humble and lowly. We know this because he chose to be born in the most humble and lowly circumstances. Indeed in choosing to be born as man, and then taking on human flesh, he was humbling himself. It is only proud sinful people that need to exalt themselves. The Word of God, who is above the highest emperor, is willing to humble himself. And in humbling himself, we come to know him as our protector and our helper. He does not cast judgement on our weaknesses, nor despise us for them. Rather he upholds and uplifts us in our weakness, so that in his strength we become strong. Yet through his humility, in choosing to be born of a human mother, we are able to see in him the pure and spotless face of the King of kings, the Supreme Ruler of the universe. His total humility is itself the sign of his supreme greatness. As we gaze on the beauty of the newborn child, we ourselves become beautiful in his image. As we look upon the light shining from that tiny baby, our dark and ignorant minds are enlightened.

Second Epistle of Clement to the Corinthians

25

Do not be irritated or angry when someone corrects you, turning you from evil to goodness. Sometimes we do wrong without knowing it because we are double-minded: we can deceive ourselves into thinking that evil is good. Equally do not be irritated or angry when you see sinful people enjoying great wealth and luxury. They are winning the contest for this world's prize, but we are running in the race for a far greater prize. The righteous person does not win his reward quickly, but must wait for it. This is because we have to train hard and long in order to win the race. After all, the crown of eternal life cannot be won easily with little effort; the person who wins it must have every spiritual muscle at the peak of fitness. It does not matter if you are weak in the affairs of commerce and trade, and so live in poverty. What matters is that you are strong in the affairs of the soul.

Second Epistle of Clement to the Corinthians

26

I send my greetings to the church in Ephesus, which is blessed with the fullness of God, and which was destined from the beginning of time to share in his eternal glory. It is God himself who has told me of your faith and love. You are true imitators of God, living according to the natural laws of righteousness which he has written in your hearts. I write to you not as someone who is superior to you, because, although I am now a slave to God, I am not yet perfect in Jesus Christ. I am learning to be a true disciple, and I look upon you as fellow learners. You can teach me much about faith and endurance. Equally my love for you prompts me to speak honestly to you about how to live in harmony with God. As a pastor, my task is to convey the will of Jesus Christ, which is the will of the Father.

Epistle of Ignatius to the Ephesians

27

It is right that you should live in harmony with the will
of the pastor, as indeed you do. The leaders amongst
you, who are truly worthy of God, are attuned to me
as their pastor like strings on a harp. So by the loving
harmony between us Jesus Christ is being sung. Let
each of you join fully in this choir, that you may
receive the note you should sing from God himself,
and so proclaim Jesus Christ with the most wonderful
spiritual music. Let the Father hear you through your
good works, and so recognize you as brothers and
sisters of his Son. The prayer of one person on his own
has great power, but the prayer of a whole church in
unity with its pastor has power beyond telling. So let
no one separate himself from the assembly, imagining
that he can do better alone; such a person is guilty of
the sin of pride. It is as humble members of a great
spiritual choir that we learn truly to love and praise
God.

Epistle of Ignatius to the Ephesians

There are some violent dogs who bark and growl at you, so you are warned of their presence; and they attack you from the front. Other violent dogs give no warning, and attack you from the rear. The latter are far more dangerous, because it is so hard to escape from their bite. The same is true of sin. Some sins are obviously wrong, and you see the temptation before it has you in its grasp. Other sins masquerade as righteousness, and bite you before you can see them for what they are; and these are far more dangerous. So how can we protect ourselves? There is only one protector and one healer: Jesus Christ. He alone can see sin for what it is, because he is divine and hence all-seeing. And, as both God and man, his flesh cannot be bitten and wounded – it cannot succumb to sin. Thus he alone can make our flesh invulnerable, so we too cannot be bitten and wounded. The means whereby our flesh takes on the properties of his flesh is the Eucharist, in which he gives his flesh for us to consume. In the Eucharist we participate in his divine flesh. The Eucharist is the medicine of salvation.

Epistle of Ignatius to the Ephesians

29

There are some who appear to be true and worthy preachers, but whose hearts are full of guile and whose minds are full of falsehood. In fact I have learned that people of this kind have actually stayed with you and preached their evil doctrine. These men are like wild beasts who attack you from behind when you are off your guard; and once you are bitten by them, it is hard to be cured. Stop your eyes to them, and chase them from your midst. And if you have been bitten, turn to Jesus Christ who is the one physician able to heal both soul and body, because he is both God and man, born of God and of Mary. To change the image, these false preachers are like hurricanes that can blow you off course. Your faith is like a windlass by which you are held on course; and your destination is the eternal love of God, which brings perfect joy. So ensure that your faith is strong, and will not break, by constant prayer and good works.

Epistle of Ignatius to the Ephesians

30

When you meet people without faith, whose lives are darkened by sin, pray for them that they may repent and find God. Ask God that your deeds of love may inspire them to become disciples. Be gentle when they are angry with you; be humble when they speak to you with contempt; respond to their blasphemy with silent prayer; remain loyal to the truth when they tell lies; be patient in the face of their cruelty, and never retaliate. Let us prove ourselves their brothers by our meekness. Remember that our Lord himself was treated with anger and contempt, he was insulted and slandered, and he suffered the most terrible cruelty; but he never flinched, firmly adhering to the will of his Father. For all their outward pride, those without faith are gripped by guilt for their sins and fear of judgement; they are prisoners of evil, bound by chains that cut into their very souls. Let us be prisoners of goodness, with Christ himself binding us with chains of spiritual pearls – pearls of loving prayer to the Father.

Epistle of Ignatius to the Ephesians

I urge you to come together frequently to give thanks and glory to God. When you gather often in God's name, the powers of Satan are destroyed, and his schemes are brought to nothing: the bonds between you become too strong for him to break. Of course you know this already because you already possess perfect faith and love, which are the beginning and the end of life: faith is the beginning, and love is the end, and when the two are joined together God is made manifest. No one who has faith commits sin, and no one who has love hates other people. As I write to you, I feel acutely the contrast between your situation and mine. I am in danger of death, you are safe; I am condemned to death, while you are vibrant with joy. Yet this contrast is superficial. Whether living or dying, whether in this world or the next, we are alive in the eternal love of our Lord Jesus. And when we meet in his name, we find new strength to face whatever trials and temptations may beset us.

Epistle of Ignatius to the Ephesians

It is better to be silent and be real, than to talk and be unreal. Teaching is good, if the teacher practices what he advises. The best teaching is not by words but by example. He who truly possesses the words of Jesus Christ in his heart hears those words constantly within the silence of his heart; and his every action expresses Christ's love. Nothing is hidden from Christ, for he can read our innermost thoughts. So let us do all things as if he were dwelling within us, that we may be his temples, and our actions become like hymns of praise. Beware of false teachers, whose mouths are filled with eloquent words, but who do not know the words of Jesus in their hearts. Only accept the teaching of those whose lives demonstrate the truth of what they are saying. Better to hear no verbal teaching at all than to risk hearing words of corruption. You who know Jesus can hear his words within your hearts, and can teach others by your actions.

Epistle of Ignatius to the Ephesians

We today are called to proclaim the birth of God's Son, Jesus Christ. But this extraordinary miracle, in which God took on human flesh, was performed in secret. It did not take place in an imperial palace, with fanfares ringing out. He was not announced from the tops of temples. Even those in the immediate vicinity did not know it was happening. It took place quietly, secretly, without fuss. There was a single outward sign of this event which transformed the world: a star shone in the sky, brighter than all other stars. Its beam was beyond description; and people remarked with astonishment at this strange new light in the sky. As it shone, it seemed that all the other stars, and the sun and the moon, became a heavenly chorus singing its praises. Some people soon became accustomed to its presence, and forgot about it. But others felt troubled by it, and wanted to discover why it had appeared. In particular some men who practised magic followed the star, and saw the child Jesus. And when they saw him, they knew that the power of their magic had been destroyed, along with all their ancient mystical arts. They fell down and glorified the new life which was displayed before them in human form.

Epistle of Ignatius to the Ephesians

Each of us, prompted by the Holy Spirit, has the right and the duty to offer guidance and advice to the church. But none of us has the right to disobey the will of the church. When we speak of obedience, people sometimes object, saying that they cannot submit themselves to any kind of human authority. We make no such demand. The authority of the church can and must be divine. And we can know that it is divine when the leaders listen carefully to the advice which people have offered, have weighed that advice, and have themselves sought divine guidance through prayer. Their decisions will not always suit our particular wishes and opinions; but, if these decisions have been reached properly, then their divine authority is assured, and we must submit to them. We are in truth not asking you to obey mere human beings; we are asking you to obey Christ himself. And in making this request, we are expecting you to act quite differently from the people of the world. They constantly want to assert themselves, in order to gain wealth and power, and satisfy their desires. We, as followers of Christ, submit ourselves, in order that the whole church may prosper.

Epistle of Ignatius to the Trallians

35

I am tempted sometimes to boast about my own knowledge of God, and to take pride in my position. But I know to give way to such temptations would prove that in truth I had nothing to boast about. It is better for me to be timid and diffident in what I say, and to ignore those whose admiring words puff me up. Those who speak to me in that way are a scourge to me. I desire to suffer for Christ's sake, but I do not know whether I am worthy to suffer. The devil is constantly at my heels, even though other people imagine me free from temptation. So I ask you to pardon me if anything I say seems motivated by pride. Indeed I believe it is when my words become complex, and I try to speak with cleverness, that pride distorts what I say. True teaching is simple, and the heart which knows the truth has no need for complex ideas. So listen to me only when I speak with simplicity.

Epistle of Ignatius to the Trallians

I pray that one day I may see you again face to face; and if Christ answers that prayer, I shall have received more than I deserve. I am frightened of the depth of the love and respect in which you hold me, because it may puff me up with pride: I might imagine myself to be the person you take me to be. You are so holy that you do the will of God with ease; but I am such a sinner that I am easily undermined. If I do see you personally, please spare me all outward signs of respect. I do not want you to be man-pleasers, but God-pleasers – as indeed you already are. If you are silent about me, giving no compliments, then I might learn to please God; but if you shower me with compliments, then the devil will be pleased. All I want is that we should be gathered together and become a great chorus of love, singing God's praises.

Epistle of Ignatius to the Romans

37

You have never envied anyone, but only taught people the way of Christ. I desire only that I may stay firmly on that way. Please pray for me, that I may have both spiritual and physical strength to perform my duties; that I may not only speak the truth, but become the truth; that I may not only be called a Christian, but also live like a Christian. Yet I do not want people to look to me as an example, for at best I can only be a pale reflection of Christ Jesus; let people look away from the reflection and turn to the reality. Christianity is not a matter of persuading people of particular ideas, but of inviting them to share in the greatness of Christ. So pray that I may never fall into the trap of impressing people with clever speech, but instead I may learn to speak with humility, desiring only to impress people with Christ himself.

Epistle of Ignatius to the Romans

I am writing to all the churches, and I am saying to all my fellow disciples that I am willing to die for God's sake. Do not show any kindness to me that would hinder this. Allow me to be eaten by wild beasts in the arena, and through the jaws of those beasts attain God's heavenly kingdom. I am God's wheat, and I want to be ground by the teeth of those beasts, and so become the pure bread of Christ. Let the wild beasts become my tomb, leaving no trace of my body, so that in death I will not cause trouble to anyone. Then when the world cannot even see my body I shall be a true disciple of Jesus Christ. Pray to Christ on my behalf that by this means I might become a sacrifice to God. I do not order you as did Peter and Paul: they were apostles, and I am a convict; they were free, and I am still a slave. But if I suffer I shall be made free, sharing in the glorious freedom of Christ's risen life.

Epistle of Ignatius to the Romans

39

I am travelling from Syria to Rome, by land and sea, by night and day, guarded by ten soldiers whom I call leopards. The more kindly I speak to these leopards, the more cruelly they treat me; and by their cruelty I am becoming a more devoted disciple of Christ. I long for the wild beasts that are prepared for me, and I pray that when I arrive I shall be taken quickly to them. Once with the beasts I shall entice them to devour me quickly; if they seem unwilling, I shall force them to it. Grant me this favour: pray that nothing will stand in the way of my suffering for Christ. I shall happily have my skin cut to shreds by the beast's teeth, my limbs torn from my body, my bones mangled in their jaws, my whole body crushed under their feet, that I may come to know Jesus. The wealth of this world counts for nothing; to be king of every nation on earth is worth no more than a few specks of dust. All that I desire is to die for the sake of the one who died for our sake.

Epistle of Ignatius to the Romans

40

The prince of this world wants to tear your souls to pieces, and turn your minds away from God towards him. Let none of you help him through deceit and hypocrisy. Do not speak warmly of Jesus Christ, and yet still lust after the things of this world. Do not let envy divide you. While in the midst of life, learn to desire death, because in that way all craving for material things will be crucified. Instead of wanting fine wine to indulge your palate, pray for the water of life to slake your spiritual thirst. Instead of wanting rich food to fill your stomach, pray for the bread of life to satisfy your spiritual hunger. Do not look for status or glory on this earth, but seek only the good opinion of God himself. Desire God alone, that he may desire you, and so guide you into his eternal kingdom. Listen to me not because I am your chosen pastor, but because as someone who is shortly to die I have no reason to deceive you; as death approaches, the truth is all that matters.

Epistle of Ignatius to the Romans

41

I perceive that your faith is settled and unshakeable. You have been firmly nailed to the cross of our Lord Jesus Christ, in flesh and in spirit. Thus as your bodily sins – greed, envy, lust – have been crucified with him, so your desires are now pure. And your spirit is free of all malice and evil thoughts, and is filled with heavenly and righteous thoughts. Those who have not been nailed to the cross firmly are beset with doubts, questioning whether Jesus Christ was truly God's Son, carping over those commandments which they find especially hard, and even quibbling over details of the account of his trial and crucifixion. They pretend that these questions are purely matters for the intellect, and must be answered by logic and reason. But their doubts arise not from the intellect, but from their souls and bodies, where the poison of sin still flows. You, by contrast, have no doubts, because the nails which pierced our Lord have also pierced you. He suffered and died for all humanity, for every single person that walks this earth. You have joined yourself to that suffering and to that death, and so you share in his promises.

Epistle of Ignatius to the Smyrnaeans

42

Some believers claim that the sufferings of our Lord
Jesus Christ were not real, but a kind of fantasy. They
argue that a man who is divine could not truly suffer;
and that they themselves, if they share in his divinity,
will also escape suffering. What they are saying is that
Christ was not truly clothed in flesh, but that his body
was a kind of corpse, a lifeless thing that gave the
appearance of a body. And this leads them to imagine
that they can enjoy the resurrection to eternal life
without sharing in the crucifixion; that their sins do
not need to be nailed on to the cross with Christ. In
fact they regard themselves as sinless. Beloved brethren,
be on your guard against these falsehoods. You may be
tempted to believe these lies, but they will lead you to
hell. Jesus Christ was born of a human mother, with a
body of flesh like ours; and in flesh he rose to life. After
his resurrection he even asked the disciples to touch
him, to prove that he was no ghost, but truly flesh.

Epistle of Ignatius to the Smyrnaeans

43

Let us imagine, as many assert, that Jesus did not rise in a physical body; but that his appearance was of a phantom. Then our faith would be in vain. We would still be subject to physical death, so the threats of our persecutors would fill us with fear and we would recant. We would be unconcerned for the physical needs of others, since Christ would have demonstrated that the body counts for nothing; we would ignore the plight of the widow, the orphan, the sick, the hungry, the thirsty, the captive – as, indeed, those who deny the physical resurrection ignore them. Equally we would be indifferent to the Eucharist, in which we receive physically the flesh and blood of Christ, because his flesh and blood would have died for ever on the cross. But we believe and we know that he rose from the tomb in body and spirit. Thus we have no fear of death, and can face our persecutors with serene courage. We commit ourselves to caring for the physical needs of the poor and the destitute. And we joyfully gather each week on the day of his resurrection to receive his flesh and his blood in the Eucharist.

Epistle of Ignatius to the Smyrnaeans

44

Those who deny the humanity of Christ Jesus also deny all human standards of morality. They are indifferent to love, they have no care for the widow and the orphan, they feel no compassion for the sick and the distressed, they see no reason to give food to the hungry and water to the thirsty, they have no concern for the prisoner. And they abstain from the Eucharist, because they deny that the Eucharist signifies the flesh of our Saviour Christ Jesus; in their eyes he had no flesh, so the Eucharist is meaningless to them. They even deny the power and purpose of prayer, because this they regard as an indulgence of the flesh; for them life in Christ is purely spiritual, so he cannot give material help in answer to prayer. These people are not in themselves wicked, for they hold their beliefs with great sincerity. But the beliefs lead to great evil and must be firmly rejected. Such people must be forbidden to speak in public and in private, and must be excluded from the fellowship.

Epistle of Ignatius to the Smyrnaeans

45

It is a great privilege for me that I have been able to meet you face to face, because your mind is like an immovable rock fixed on God. I urge you to stay firm in your faith, because as a pastor you give such strength to the faith of others. Ensure that all the congregations in your care remain unified in Christ, because unity is Christ's deepest desire. Love all people as the Lord loves you. Be disciplined in your prayer. Ask constantly for greater wisdom, and never let your soul slumber. Speak to each person with the same respect as you speak to God, because the Spirit of God is in all people. Do not be afraid of hard work, because where the toil is hardest the gain is greatest. It is no credit to you to give attention to the good and faithful disciples; concentrate your efforts on those who are wayward and troublesome, winning them for Christ with your gentleness. Remember that as sailors require wind, so you require the guidance of the Holy Spirit; and just as in a storm sailors need a safe harbour, so in times of difficulty the Holy Spirit will calm your soul. So with the Holy Spirit behind and within you, your work as a pastor will bring great blessing to your congregations and to you.

Epistle of Ignatius to Polycarp

46

Do not neglect the widows; be their guardian and their protector. Indeed protect all who are weak and vulnerable, because they enjoy the special favour of God. Ensure that you know the name of everyone in your congregations. Do not look down on slaves, whether male or female, but treat everyone with equal respect, because God loves all people equally. Encourage your congregations to meet frequently for worship and for fellowship, that they may be filled with love for God and for one another. Preach firmly and without compromise against any evil practices, even if they seem quite trivial and harmless; the devil works by gaining small victories. Teach wives to be content with their husbands, both in flesh and in spirit, and husbands to be content with their wives; and if they have the strength, let them learn to live together without sexual activity, that they may devote themselves fully to God. And those who wish to marry should seek your consent, to ensure they are marrying not for lust but for the Lord.

Epistle of Ignatius to Polycarp

47

Urge your congregations to listen to your words, not because you personally have any special wisdom, but because the Lord has appointed you as their guide on earth, and so his Spirit speaks through you. And let your teaching be simple. Urge them to see themselves as one body, the body of Christ; and as a single body their task on earth is to become like an athlete, able to use his natural strength to the full. Thus as different parts of Christ's body, they must use the gifts that God has bestowed on them to the full, serving one another with all their strength. Let them also see themselves as a soldier, with faith their helmet, love their spear, and endurance their armour. Indeed using such simple images, you will be able to convey to them the life they should lead while on earth. And in the manner of your teaching exude the joy which is ours in Christ Jesus; because when our hearts are firmly rooted in the joy of Christ, then all things become possible, and no physical or mental suffering is too much to bear.

Epistle of Ignatius to Polycarp

In truth I know that you have little need of my advice, because I know from numerous reports that the church in Antioch enjoys great peace and harmony, through the power of your teaching and your prayer. It is you who should be encouraging and guiding me, who remains a poor sinner. I long to be free of my cares and duties on this earth, and to enjoy the eternal freedom of the resurrection; and in seeking this eternal freedom I regard myself as your disciple. Dear Polycarp, I ask you to summon a meeting of those for whom you have the highest regard; and appoint from that group someone who is a fervent disciple of Christ, to act as God's courier to me. Let that person come to me, to act as my brother and my mentor. I realize that I have no power over myself, but need the support of a true Christian friend. Such a favour to me would be a true work of God. In the meantime I bid you farewell in the name of our Lord Jesus Christ; may you remain unified in him, enjoying the boundless love of God.

Epistle of Ignatius to Polycarp

49

I rejoice greatly with you in our Lord Jesus Christ, that you have followed the pattern of true love, and have helped one another in the ways of righteousness, as opportunity has arisen. Once you were prisoners of sin, now you are jewels in the crown of life. I rejoice too that you have remained firmly rooted in the faith for so many years. Your initial spiritual fervour when the seed was first sown was famous throughout the world. Now that seed has grown into a strong, robust tree bearing succulent spiritual fruit. And this fruit attracts newcomers to taste it, so they too come to enjoy the rich grace of our Lord. I write to you now not because I am worthy to offer you guidance, but because you have invited me to write. I cannot emulate the wisdom of the apostle Paul who taught you so accurately the truth about Christ, both in speech when he was amongst you, and in letters when he was absent. It is better that you study his words, which will build up your faith, than pay attention to what I can write.

Epistle of Polycarp to the Philippians

Remember that we bring nothing into this world, and can take nothing out. So we should put no trust in material riches, but only in spiritual treasures; and metal armour cannot save us from evil, but only the armour of righteousness. Those of you who are wives should love your husbands not with lust but with gentle concern for their spiritual well-being; and you should educate your children in the fear of God. Those of you who are widows have a special opportunity to give the same chaste love that you once directed to your husbands to the whole church. Let the husbands amongst you protect your wives from all evil, be firm in directing your sons and daughters in the way of righteousness, and be examples of spiritual strength to all. And all of you should avoid slander, false witness, love of money, and every kind of evil. For each of you is an altar on which every action, every thought and every feeling is offered as a sacrifice to God.

Epistle of Polycarp to the Philippians

51

Let your pastors be blameless in all matters, temperate, compassionate, scrupulously honest, and the servant of everyone. What you do for God in the world you shall receive back from him a hundredfold in the life to come. Your duty as a pastor is to bring back those whose minds and hearts have wandered from the truth, to care for the weak and vulnerable, to ensure that the poor amongst you have ample food and clothing, and in all things to treat everyone with equal love and respect. Do not be hasty in judgement, or quick to show anger, but be patient and calm, trusting always in the judgement and the power of God. Day by day pray to God to forgive you for the ways in which you failed in your duties, asking him for greater strength in the future. And as soon as you become aware of an error or sin you have committed, do not try to hide it, but confess it openly, asking the forgiveness of those in your care.

Epistle of Polycarp to the Philippians

52

Christ is our hope, and in that hope we find courage to persevere through all trials, temptations and hardships. Let us imitate the endurance of Christ, who suffered and died for our sake. Remember Ignatius, Zosimus and Rufus, as well as Paul himself, who suffered and died for their faith in Christ. They did not run the course of life in vain, but in death they received the crown of glory. When you feel weak in the faith, draw closer together for mutual support, that together you may be strong. When your mind becomes distracted by worldly concerns, concentrate your attention on the needs of others, and work even harder to satisfy those needs. Above all, do not allow your faith to be perverted by false teaching. There are always people who are prepared to pervert the words of Christ for their own purposes, and to deny the final judgement in order to persuade themselves and others that they can sin without fear of punishment. Do not even listen to such people, but turn your back on them.

Epistle of Polycarp to the Philippians

53

I am deeply sorry for Valens, who was once a leader amongst you, but who did not understand the task to which he had been called. Instead he used his position for personal gain, and had to be excluded from your fellowship; now he is lost in the darkness of ignorance and loneliness. Learn from his example. Perform the tasks assigned to you with purity of motive and with honesty of intention. If you make money your purpose, then money becomes your god, and you its slave. Both Valens and his wife are now slaves to money, and I pray daily that they may repent and receive God's forgiveness, and so return to the flock. But happily avarice and greed are now alien to you, and by all reports you labour for Christ with the same diligence which you showed when the apostle Paul was amongst you. Do not regard Valens and his wife as enemies, but rather as fallible human beings who have gone astray. You too are fallible and could go astray without constant attention to the truth. The lesson you must learn from their example is to remain always vigilant in your devotion to the Lord.

Epistle of Polycarp to the Philippians

54

I know that you are well versed in the Scriptures, and nothing in the sacred texts escapes your notice. I only wish the same was true of me. Let that knowledge of the Scriptures be your foundation, on which the magnificent edifice of faith is built. And let the stones of that edifice be honesty, gentleness, serenity, patience, long-suffering, endurance and purity. May it become a great spiritual palace, that evokes admiration and even envy in all who see it. It is in a spirit of admiring envy that I write this letter; I wish I could share fully your glorious faith. I know that my letter is worthless, but I enclose for your benefit the letter which Ignatius sent to me, and from which I have gained much strength. His letter expresses the very qualities with which your palace of faith is being built. I ask you in return to send to me any words you yourself had from Ignatius, so that I may be further uplifted by him.

Epistle of Polycarp to the Philippians

55

Greetings, sons and daughters of the almighty Father;
may his love and peace be with you. I rejoice at the
generous and warm-hearted spirit, which God has
instilled within you; you have truly been born anew in
his love. When I look upon you, and see the glorious
blessings which God pours out on those who are saved,
I congratulate myself on my own salvation; the sight of
you is the promise of what I will become. Since I was
with you I feel the Lord has travelled with me on my
journeys, guiding my feet in the way of righteousness.
And as I have come to know the Lord a little better, I
have grown to love you even more dearly, cherishing
you above my own life. And out of that love I want to
share with you some of the insights which I have
received – hence this short letter. It is a privilege for
me to be able to minister to such noble spirits as yours.

Epistle of Barnabas

56

There are three central aspects of Christianity. The first is the hope of eternal life, which is the beginning and end of our faith. The second is righteousness, which is the beginning and end of judgement. The third is joy, which is the beginning and end of love. Through the resurrection of Jesus Christ, we have had a glimpse of what is promised for all who are saved, because he is the first-fruits of the harvest of salvation. Through the example of Jesus Christ in his life and work, we understand righteousness, and by following his example we can be sure of favourable judgement. Through the joy which Jesus mediates, which originates in his perfect heart of love, we want to share that joy, and so grow in his love. We live in evil days, and the prince of evil is in power in the world. Thus we need to hold fast to our hope, our righteousness and our joy, granted to us by God in Christ, that we may resist all evil, and finally rise to eternal life.

Epistle of Barnabas

In these last days our life and our faith will profit us nothing unless, as sons and daughters of God, we can ensure that the Evil One has no entry into our hearts or our fellowship. Let us avoid all vanity, because it is by appealing to our sense of pride that the Evil One can more easily seduce us. Do not try to live alone, away from your fellow disciples, as if you were already righteous; instead stay close to each other, because together your spiritual strength is multiplied. Strive to keep the commandments of Christ with punctilious precision, never trying to make excuses or exceptions, because only in this way can you stay on the straight and narrow path that leads to eternal life. No matter what your position or status is on earth, you will be judged by the same standards as everyone else, because God is no respecter of worldly status. Be constantly vigilant: do not rest content with yourself as you are, but night and day strive to be more like Christ. The person who slumbers in his sin will die in sin; the person awake to righteousness will live in righteousness.

Epistle of Barnabas

We have been created anew in Christ Jesus; our hearts of stone have become hearts of flesh. In truth Jesus himself lives within our hearts, so our bodies become temples of his Spirit. And he also lives amongst us, binding us together in love. In days of old the Hebrew people were promised a land of milk and honey. We have now received the true and eternal milk and honey. A child is first nourished with milk, and then with honey. In the same way Christ nourishes us with spiritual milk when we first come to faith, feeding us the aspects of the truth that we can understand. Then he begins to feed us the spiritual honey of divine joy, pouring his love into our souls until we are overflowing with praise and thanksgiving. Yet like a loving parent, God not only feeds us, but also guides and disciplines us, showing his anger when we do wrong, so our souls are filled with remorse. God rules over the birds, and the wild animals, the flowers and the trees, showing his love for them by determining how they should grow and live. His love for us is far greater, so his commands are far stricter.

Epistle of Barnabas

As far as possible, and as simply as possible, let me try to summarize what is necessary for salvation. I do not want to write in parables, but in plain words. There are two ways: the way of light, and the way of darkness. And there is a great difference between these two ways. Along the way of light stand the angels of God, radiating his brightness. Along the way of darkness stand the angels of Satan, casting their shadows over the path. The way of light goes from eternity to eternity; the way of darkness from iniquity to iniquity. To follow the way of light a person must study carefully the commandments of God, and follow them precisely. Anyone who does this shall enjoy the eternal light that shines from God's throne, because for all eternity he shall sit in God's presence, basking in his light, and praising his glory. But anyone who follows the way of darkness shall perish.

Epistle of Barnabas

The way of light is a journey to a destination chosen by God. And to make that journey you must follow God's directions, which are these. You shall love and fear God as your creator; and you shall glorify him as the one who redeemed you from death. You shall be simple in heart and rich in spirit. You shall not mix with those who work in the way of death, and you shall hate all that is not pleasing to God. You shall reject men who are hypocritical, and you shall always be honest and sincere. You shall not try to exalt yourself, or take any glory to yourself for what you achieve, but be humble, boasting only in God's power. You shall not make malicious plans against your neighbour. In your conversation you shall never say things contrary to God's Word, but always affirm God's Word, even if this provokes hostility. You shall be indifferent to men's status, opposing sin wherever you find it and whoever commits it. You shall be meek and quiet, listening carefully to everything men say, in order to discern God's wisdom in their words.

Epistle of Barnabas

61

If you wish to follow the way of light, you shall love
your neighbour more than your own life. You shall
cherish your sons and daughters, teaching them to love
and fear God. You shall not abort the unborn child in
order to avoid the duties of parenthood, nor murder
infants, but rejoice in every child as a gift from God.
You shall not be greedy and envy your neighbour's
possessions. You shall not seek out powerful and
wealthy men as your friends, but prefer instead the
friendship of the humble and the righteous. Whatever
suffering and hardships befall you in the course of life,
you shall accept these as sent by God, knowing that
nothing happens without God. You shall not be two-
faced or unduly talkative. You shall obey those in
authority over you, so long as what they command is
in accordance with God's commands. And you shall be
gentle and merciful in giving commands to those under
your authority, since servant and master are equal in
God's sight, with the same hope of salvation.

Epistle of Barnabas

If you wish to reach the destination God has appointed for you, then you shall regard nothing in your possession as belonging to you, but everything as belonging to God. Thus you shall be willing to share all things with your neighbour, knowing that your reward shall be spiritual wealth that can never rust or decay. You shall not push forward your own opinions, but seek in all matters to discern the will of God. You shall love and cherish as the apple of your eye all who speak to you about God, guiding you along the way of light. Day and night you shall remember that life on earth is a preparation for the life to come; and thus you shall live and act day and night in the anticipation of God's judgement. When opportunities arise to help others, you shall not grumble, but rejoice in the prospect of pleasing God. You shall avoid all quarrels over earthly matters, but work together with others in earning God's approval. You shall never worship God with an evil conscience, but always confess any sins and make amends before worshipping God, so you can come to him with a pure heart. This is the way of light.

Epistle of Barnabas

63

The way of darkness is crooked, leading to everlasting punishment; and along it are all the things that destroy the soul. Those who follow the way of darkness worship their own wealth and fame and power; they luxuriate in their superiority over others, imagining themselves to be like gods. They are hypocrites, impressing people with their virtue and presenting themselves to the world as benevolent and generous, yet all the while trying to gather more money and to manipulate people for their own ends. They are like brutes in their own homes, treating their wives like slaves, and they feel free to satisfy their lusts with other women. They are proud, enjoying the sound of their own voices and ignoring the wisdom and insights of others. If it suits their purposes, they will make malicious plans against those who imagine themselves to be friends; and they will feel no remorse at the suffering and humiliation they cause to their friends. They become so accustomed to telling lies that they cannot distinguish even in their own minds between truth and falsehood.

Epistle of Barnabas

64

Those who follow the way of darkness cannot worship God, so they put their trust in magic and astrology. Despite their outward arrogance, their hearts are full of fear about the future; so they try to predict the future by reading the stars, and change the future by casting spells. And despite the pleasure they take in doing others down, their hearts are lonely and miserable; so they use magic in order to find for themselves someone they can truly love. Yet the power of God is always greater than the power of magic; and true love can only be enjoyed as a gift of God, to those who have given their heart to him. So those who follow the way of darkness can never escape the cold fear and loneliness that grips their hearts. And the fear and loneliness keep them awake in the long dark hours of the night. In the daytime they smile and laugh, as if they owned the world, but at night the horrible truth of their condition cannot be avoided. This is the way of darkness.

Epistle of Barnabas

65

On the way of darkness the black skies echo to the sounds of blasphemy. Those who work on that way, while claiming to be indifferent to God, must force themselves to hate him, in order to pursue their evil purposes. They shudder at the thought of caring for small children, because the innocence of children is an accusation against their impurity; so they urge their wives to abort their unborn babies, and they will order their own infant sons and daughters to be murdered; and if even they cannot bring themselves to such depths of cruelty they will ignore their children, as if they did not exist. As for showing charity to widows and orphans from other families, it is unthinkable to them; they are without compassion or pity. They look upon the trees and plants, the animals and birds which God has created with equal contempt. They see no beauty in what God has made, but only the means to satisfy their greedy desires and lusts. So when they see a lush valley they want to possess it and exploit its fertility to add to their own wealth, rather than to share its beauty and its bounty with others.

Epistle of Barnabas

I have written to you very fully and frankly about the ways of light and darkness because I want your eyes to be open and awake. I know that all of you want to follow the way of light, in order to receive the glorious reward that God promises to those who are saved; so you must be vigilant in keeping to its path, and not straying into the way of darkness out of ignorance or carelessness. For those who stay in the light there is resurrection; for those who live in the darkness there is punishment. Those of you who are pastors, enjoying spiritual authority over others, must set an example; if you stumble, you may cause many others to stumble with you. But in truth all of you have authority over one another, because all of you have spiritual gifts and insights which should be used to guide one another. So each of you must set an example to the others. As for me, I ask you constantly to pray for me, that despite my own natural ignorance and carelessness, my eyes may always be open to the glorious light of God, and I may always have the courage to work in his way of light.

Epistle of Barnabas

Since I perceive, most excellent Diognetus, that you are exceedingly eager to learn the religion of the Christians, and are asking very clear and careful questions about them, I must respond. You have asked who is the God in whom they believe; how they worship him; why they show such disregard for the things of the world and are happy to die; why they reject as idols those who are considered gods by the Greeks, and also reject the superstitions of the Jews; what is the nature of the love which binds them together; and why this new religion has sprung up at this time, and not before. I welcome and admire this eagerness in you to learn about the Christian religion; and I ask God, who gives the power both of speaking and of hearing, that he may guide me to speak and you to hear in such a way that it will be of great benefit to you. And if what you hear in any way upsets or offends you, I ask your forgiveness.

Epistle to Diognetus

68

Please clear yourself of all prejudice which mists your mind, and throw aside the traditional attitudes which deceive you, and become like a child who is about to listen to a new story. Look, not only with your eyes but also with your intelligence, at those entities which you call gods. What is their form; what is their substance? Is not one a stone, like the stones on which we walk; another a lump of bronze, no different from the vessels in which we carry water; another wood, which is already rotting; another silver, requiring a man to guard it against theft; another iron, eaten by rust; another earthenware, no more beautiful than the plates on which we eat our meals? Are they not all made of perishable materials? Were they not forged by iron and fire? Did not the woodcarver make one, the brass-founder another, the silversmith another, the potter another? Before they were moulded into their present shapes, was it not possible that they could have been given different shapes? Are they not all dumb, blind, without feelings, without souls, without movement? Do you call these things gods? Are these what you serve? While you praise these lifeless objects, and vow to serve them, the Christians despise them, and despise what you are doing.

Epistle to Diognetus

69

I think you are especially anxious to hear why Christians do not worship in the same way as Jews. As you know, the Jews reject the worship of idols, and believe in one God of the entire universe, regarding him as their Master. Since Christians also believe in one God, Jews and Christians are similar. But just as Greeks offer sacrifices and gifts to their idols, so the Jews offer sacrifices and gifts to God, as if he needed these things. In doing this they show foolishness, not reverence. He who made heaven and earth and all that is in them, and bestows on us all that we need, has no need of gifts from us; after all, to offer gifts and sacrifices of blood and burnt fat to God we are doing nothing better than the Greeks who offer blood and burnt fat to idols; both activities are utterly pointless. God needs nothing from us; it is we who are utterly dependent on him.

Epistle to Diognetus

70

I doubt if you need to learn from me that the Jewish scruples about food, their superstitions about the sabbath, their pride in circumcision, and their fasting and feasting according to the phases of the moon, are ridiculous and irrational. When God has created every type of food, how can it be right to reject some types of food as unclean? When God has created us to do good and to express love, how can it be right to refuse to do a good deed on the sabbath? And to take pride in mutilating the flesh, as if this in itself gained God's special favour and proved that they were chosen by him, is just laughable. As for their attention to the stars and moon, and for their arbitrary selection of days for fasting and feasting, this is not a proof of piety, but of folly. So Christians refrain from such silliness and deceit, and they avoid all fussiness and pride.

Epistle to Diognetus

The distinction between Christians and other people lies not in country or language or customs. Christians do not dwell in special houses or districts of cities, nor do they use a peculiar dialect, nor do they have any extraordinary customs. Their teaching has not been discovered by the intellect of clever men, nor do they advocate any human doctrine. Wherever they live they follow the local customs, eating the food that local people eat, living in ordinary houses, and wearing clothes indistinguishable from those of their neighbours. It is in their attitudes that they are distinctive. They live in the lands where they were born, but see themselves not as owners of that land, but as sojourners; they are strangers on this earth. To them every foreign land is like their fatherland, and every fatherland like a foreign land. They behave as perfect and upright citizens, according to the laws of whatever state they inhabit; but they see themselves as citizens of another state, the kingdom of God.

Epistle to Diognetus

Christians marry as other people do and they bear children; but they cherish their off-spring as children of God. They offer hospitality freely, but they do not allow visitors to corrupt their way of life. They have bodies like all human beings, but they are not slaves to bodily cravings. They obey the laws of the State, but in their own lives they are subservient to far higher laws. They love all men, even when they are despised by all men. They lead secret lives, never flaunting their faith and holiness, and yet attract such attention and such anger that they cannot escape persecution. When they are put to death, they gain eternal life. They regard themselves as rich in God's blessings, even when materially they are poor. When they are treated with contempt they glory in that contempt; and when people speak evil of them, their confidence in God's approval of them is boosted. When people treat them badly, they bless those people and want to help them. Jews hate them as traitors and Greeks persecute them as subversives, yet no one can justify this enmity.

Epistle to Diognetus

To put it succinctly, what the soul is within the body, Christians are within the world. The soul is spread through all parts of the body, and Christians throughout all the cities of the world. The soul dwells in the body, but is not of the body; in the same way Christians live in the world, but are not of the world. The soul is invisible, and is guarded by a visible body; the Christian religion is invisible, yet Christians are recognised in the world for what they are. The flesh tries to corrupt the soul by making the soul a slave to its desires; so the world tries to corrupt Christians by making them renounce their faith and adopt the world's values. The soul loves the flesh which hates it; Christians love the people who hate them. The soul is enclosed in the body and thence sustains it; Christians are confined within the world, and the world is sustained by their prayers. The soul when it withstands temptation becomes stronger; Christians by withstanding persecution become more numerous.

Epistle to Diognetus

Christian doctrine is not based on some earthly discovery, nor is it based on a process of rational deduction. Equally the Christian doctrine is not a mystery which only people of great intellect can understand. It is given by the almighty and all-creating God, who has implanted his Word in their hearts. He did this by sending his own agent, who had been the instrument by which he created the heavens and the earth, into the world in human form. This agent had at the beginning of time set the sun and moon on their courses, enclosed the sea in its bounds, fashioned the mountains and the valleys, and brought every living creature into existence. You might imagine that when this agent took human form, he might strike terror into people's hearts. On the contrary, he was meek and gentle, a man amongst men, who won their hearts not by force, but by persuasion. He did not pursue people, but called them. He did not judge them, but loved them. He did not threaten them, but blessed them.

Epistle to Diognetus

God planned to send this Child as our saviour from the beginning of time. But until recently he allowed us to be ruled by our desires, and carried along by our lusts. He did this not because he delighted in our sins, but in patience and forbearance. He wanted to give us ample chance to repent of our sins of our own accord, and turn away from iniquity to righteousness. But when we had made it plain that by ourselves we could not enter his kingdom, he decided that he must give us the power to repent. And at the moment when our sins had plumbed the lowest depths of depravity, and we deserved only punishment, then by his overflowing love he came to our rescue. He could not stand by and watch us destroying ourselves, and took pity on us, sending his Son as a ransom for our sin. He offered his Son as an innocent man in exchange for the guilty, a just man in exchange for the unjust, an incorruptible man in exchange for the corrupt, an immortal man in exchange for those doomed by their sins to death.

Epistle to Diognetus

What else could cover our sins but the divine righteousness of God's Son? How else could our sins be wiped clean except by God's Son taking upon himself our punishment? What a sweet exchange! What a wonderful event! What undeserved blessings! What a miracle that our wickedness should be absorbed by the One who is perfectly righteous, making us righteous! God allowed us to remain in the mire of our sin for so long to prove to us that in our own strength we could not lift ourselves. And when we were convinced that we needed help – when pride in our strength had been finally destroyed by our desperate plight – then he sent the greatest help that he could, in the form of his Son. Now a person only has to turn towards God's Son, and God's Son reaches down and lifts that person out of the mire of sin, onto the firm and solid ground of righteousness. And God's Son becomes to all those who turn to him their nurse, teacher, brother, counsellor, physician and saviour, giving them strength, wisdom, love, comfort, power and glory.

Epistle to Diognetus

77

If you also desire this faith, and so come to know God as your Father, then you need only turn towards his Son. God created this world out of love for humanity, putting all things under human dominion; and he gave us the faculty of reason, by which we can exercise our dominion with justice and care. And in giving us reason, he was fashioning us in his own image, for God possesses supreme and perfect reason. Yet in our sinfulness our image became distorted, and we failed to use our reason justly and carefully. Then God sent his Son to reveal himself, and thus show us the image of how he created us and how he wishes to restore us. So when you turn to God's Son you know who you truly are, and how your true nature can be restored. And when you come to know your true self through God's Son, you shall be filled with joy beyond imagination, because you shall know the completeness of God's love for you and for all people.

Epistle to Diognetus

When you come to know God's love in your heart, you will want to express that love in your life, following the example of God's Son. Indeed you will want to imitate God, because he has created you in his image. You may think it is impossible for a man to imitate God; but when a man truly wants this, it is possible. And imitating God brings true happiness. People often imagine that happiness consists in dominating one's neighbours, in exerting power over people weaker than oneself, in acquiring wealth, in having numerous slaves, in opposing the poor. But these things are quite contrary to God's love, and bring misery to their perpetrators. Happiness consists in helping one's neighbour, in sharing the material bounty which God gives, in setting slaves free, in uplifting the poor. A person who does these things is a true imitator of God, and receives the reward of divine joy even on this earth.

Epistle to Diognetus

Once you start to imitate God here on earth, then you will realise that your soul already lives in heaven, and you will thus begin to understand the mysteries of God. You will love and admire those who are being persecuted because they refuse to deny God. You will condemn the deceit and error of this world. You will hold even death itself in contempt, because you will know that true life is to be found in heaven. You will become fearless in speaking to others about God, because no punishment inflicted by earthly powers can extinguish the divine joy in your heart. Thus the prospect of being thrown to wild beasts, and being burnt at the stake, will not strike terror in your heart, but will be a matter of indifference. You will find yourself thanking God for everything that befalls you, whether it brings pain or pleasure, because you will trust God completely. Do you not think that to imitate God, and become such a person, is the life that all wise and rational men should adopt?

Epistle to Diognetus

I am writing to you plainly, without resorting to strange words or ideas, because I am a disciple of the apostles. They were men who heard the teachings of God's Son, and were commissioned by him to spread those teachings across the world. Thus they had to speak in ways that ordinary people, with no special knowledge, could comprehend. I try to be their worthy successor; and if you can comprehend what I am saying, then I am satisfied. And for your part if you espouse the Christian religion you too shall be an apostle for God's Son. You will recall how you came from ignorance to knowledge, and you will be able to lead others along the same path. To be a successor to the apostles is the most wonderful honour and the most joyful task. It is sometimes tempting to use strange words, in order to impress others with one's cleverness. But to follow the Christian religion does not require cleverness in the human sense. On the contrary the truth which God's Son taught is simple, such that anyone can understand it. It is not cleverness but humility which is required to grasp the truth.

Epistle to Diognetus

If you listen to the truth, and consider it carefully, you will understand that God invites those who love him into a paradise of joy. He plants within them a seed, which grows up into a beautiful tree, bearing every kind of fruit, with each fruit more sweet and succulent than the last. Amongst these fruits are two of particular importance. One is knowledge and the other is life. Knowledge is not concerned with facts or with the kind of speculation beloved of philosophers. Rather it consists in accepting the Word of God, conveyed by God's Son; and through acceptance, coming to understand its meaning and penetrate its mystery. Life is not concerned with worldly activities and achievements, nor with the pursuit of pleasure, which most people see as the purpose of our existence. Rather it consists in purity of motive and intention, which alone can lead to the kind of actions which God desires. These two fruits are to be found at the very top of the tree that grows within the soul. And each depends on the other: without life there cannot be knowledge; and without knowledge there cannot be life.

Epistle to Diognetus

Knowledge separated from life causes spiritual pride. There are many people, calling themselves disciples of God's Son, who study the Christian religion, and fill their minds with all sorts of information about God. They imagine that this knowledge makes them holy, and they enjoy displaying their knowledge to others, to give the impression of holiness. With such people knowledge has been turned from a sweet, succulent fruit into something bitter and poisonous, for pride in one's own knowledge destroys the soul. Knowledge can only be sweet and succulent, nourishing the soul, if it is put into practice in daily life. Indeed knowledge of God teaches us to serve others, helping the weak, comforting the sick, and feeding the hungry. If we study God's Word, but refuse to obey it, we are making a mockery of God. And he in turn will punish us. Far from being holy, we shall find ourselves miserable, our hearts empty of love, and our souls deprived of any joy. So when you begin to acquire knowledge of the religion of the Christians, make sure you put that knowledge into practice, or else it would be better to remain ignorant.

Epistle to Diognetus

Life separated from knowledge lacks any direction or purpose. The person who wants to follow the Christian religion, but is too lazy to learn its teachings, will find himself living no differently from those without faith. The fruit of life will become dry and wizened, containing no nourishment for the soul. There are many people who hear about the Christian religion, and whose hearts are seized with enthusiasm; they imagine they can imitate God's Son immediately, without studying his teachings and thinking out how to apply those teachings to their own situation. But if religion was simply a matter of enthusiasm, which can show itself in lively exuberance, God's Son would not have been so full and so detailed in the precepts he gave us. The person who wishes to follow the Christian religion must learn the teachings of Jesus and his apostles, studying them daily, and devoting time each day to silent reflection, thinking out what these teachings mean in his own circumstances. So if you want to become a disciple of God's Son, remember that you must apply your mind vigorously to what he taught; and you must continue as a pupil of God's Son until the day you die.

Epistle to Diognetus

God has already planted his seed in your heart. You do not have to look for it or ask for it; you can find it already inside you. His Son will water it with his teaching so it germinates and grows. And the love which radiates from his Son will give it warmth to bring forth blossoms and then fruit. Then as the tree of faith reaches its full height, the fruits of true knowledge and true life will appear. All this is possible. For it to happen you must turn to God's Son and ask him to water God's seed with his teachings, to warm your heart with his love, and so let his sweet and succulent fruits grow inside you. God is now urging you to do this, and he is using me as his instrument to speak to you. As I write, it is God who is guiding my hand. And as you read, it is God who is trying to speak to you. Listen, and be saved. Take heed, and share in God's eternal joy.

Epistle to Diognetus

FURTHER READING

The Early Christian Fathers
A selection from the writings of the Fathers from St Clement of Rome to St Athanasius
Edited and translated by Henry Bettenson
Oxford: Oxford University Press, 1969

The Apostolic Fathers (2 volumes)
Translated by Kirsopp Lake
Loeb Classical Library
London: William Heinemann Ltd, 1985

Early Christian Writings: The Apostolic Fathers
Translated by Maxwell Stamforth
Revised and introduced by Andrew Louth
London: Penguin Classics, 1987

The Apostolic Fathers (2nd edition)
Translated by JB Lightfoot and JR Harmer
Edited and revised by Michael W Holmes
Leicester: Apollos, 1990